Acknowledgements
My special thanks to the following people

Monsignor Philip Shryane, VG, my parish priest, for his guidance and help on all things spiritual.

Larry A. King for the Voice of Missions, USA, for his support in promoting the book overseas and for his review.

Maggie Secker, BBC Radio Norfolk, for allowing me to guest on Maggie's Brew and for her encouragement with my writing.

Sister Mary-Richard, IBVM, of St George's Parish, for her constructive criticism regarding my usage of grammar, and for proof-reading the text.

Janet Fuller, my sister-in-law, and her husband, Mike, for all their help on so many occasions.

Jean and Gerald Newton, my cousins, for always believing that I could complete this daunting project.

Diana Mazzoni, for allowing me to bounce my ideas off her, and for her cheerful support on my bad hair days!

Tim Hunt, product manager, Jarrold Publishing, for his professional help in bringing the book to print stage and Kaarin Wall, freelance designer, for her superb flair and invaluable help with the ultimate design work.

Dedications

To my husband, Keith,
and my daughters, Tracey and Rosie,
who in various ways have encouraged
and supported me towards the fulfilment
of my dream to publish this book.

Foreword

We often speak of being moved by music, by great works of art or beautiful scenery; perhaps we think of words in a more mundane way. Sometimes words too, can move us to the very core of our being or strike deep chords for us, especially words of poetry and faith. When we speak or write, we usually know what our words will do, maybe encourage or perhaps criticise, but we cannot always be sure how they are heard. In these words Anne Monument will certainly uplift, support and encourage a great many people in a huge variety of circumstances about which she will never know.

Anne's poetry is natural and very appealing. It comes from a heart full of faith in the goodness and love of God. Much of the poetry catches something of the everyday and then, with a beautiful twist, links to the wonder and abiding presence of God in your everyday. Anne has been a parishioner of mine for over ten years and it has been a joy to see her faith grow and develop through years which have brought all kinds of difficulties and obstacles in her own life, but through which there is always a shining faith and deep confidence in a God who is both close and very real. I am sure that you will enjoy this book, and whether you have a faith or not, it will, I know, speak to you as it did to me, of comfort and of hope.

Monsignor Philip Shryane, VG
Parish Priest

Contents

The Sparkle on the Ground 11
Perseverance 12
Help! 13
The Touch of Time 14
Nature's Balm 16
Forward Movement 17
My Daughter 18
And I, your Mother 20
What we install… 21
A Thump in the Night 22-23
Insight 24
St Jude 27
Murphy's Law 28
The Blessing of St Jude 29
Gossamer Threads 30-31
What we say… 32
On Being Called
    Platitudinous! 33
The Leap of Faith 35
Hugs 36
The Hug 37
The Vase 38-39
Finding God 41
Witness 42
Each one of us… 43
Marriage is 44
Warts and All 47
Canine Perspective 48
Friendship 50
An acquaintance is someone… 51

An Image of Thee 53
I'm Not Superstitious, Are You?
    54-55
The Tapestry 56
No Strings Attached 58
Gratitude 59
Gifts from Above 61
The Candlelight of Prayer 62-63
Time saved 65
Sometimes in life… 66
Experience 68
In the bank account… 69
Job's Story 70-73
Forgiveness 74
In order to be forgiven… 75
What's in a Number? 76
Full Circle 77
The Gift of Foster Parents 78-79
A Prayer at Work 80
A Prayer for Help 80
A Family Prayer at Night 80
Retirement Prayer 81
Practise to Make Perfect 82
Laughter 83
Jonah's Story 84-87
Alone But Not Lonely 88
Receiving Graciously 89
My Glimpse of Eternity 90-91
Epilogue 92
An abridged autobiography! 93

The Sparkle on the Ground

Shivering on a shingle beach,
Almost too cold to stay,
Watching the waves on grey-brown stones,
Their groping fingers play.
I thought the landscape dull and drear,
But then I looked again,
Seeing a stone of different hue,
Amongst the others lain.
The light was sombre, yet it gleamed
Outshining all the rest,
And then I noticed smaller stones,
In twinkling splendour dressed.

I thought about the lives we lead,
And how in haste we miss,
Amid the seeming dreariness,
A moment of pure bliss.
We fail to see in others too,
If all we do is glance,
Their beauty and their goodness,
That is waiting for a chance.
I thought about a truth that day,
As I was homeward bound,
We miss so much if we don't watch,
For the sparkle on the ground!

Perseverance

Never give up and don't despair,
For nearly and nearly you are almost there.
You may not have just all that you need,
But surely and surely you will succeed.

Never give up, don't fall at the fence,
Though the hurdles you jump may be immense.
You may not feel that life is much fun,
But surely and surely the race is won.

Never give up and don't lose heart,
For each life experience plays its part.
You may not see the whole picture yet,
But surely and surely the scene is set.

Never give up on each of your dreams,
Even with tattered and jagged seams.
For just when you feel a cause for despair,
Surely and surely you'll find you are there.

Help!

Give me a break today, dear Lord,
Is all I ask,
For every simple task,
Seems hard to do.
Demanding kids are late for school,
Spouse late for work,
Whilst rumbling crises lurk,
At every turn.

Give me a break today, dear Lord,
An inner peace,
Amid the elbow grease
And daily grind.
Through dusting, washing, multi-chores,
Amid discord,
Teach me to praise the Lord,
When on my knees.

The Touch of Time

Empty my nest with fledgling flown,
Only a moment since first teeth were cut
In dribbling misery.
Neat map of life set out before me then,
The walking, talking, everyday,
The sharing things.
First child, a blessing and a curse,
It seemed forever you would stay,
In knowing, growing, joined togetherness.
But time crept up,
Stalked stealthily its prey,
So suddenly the fledgling child had grown.

Pervading piercing pain of parting,
Great chunk of me dissected and removed,
Raw and exposed.
No map, just yawning crater to infill,
With walking, talking, everyday,
Not sharing things.
Insatiable this emptiness inside,
It seemed forever it would stay.
Until a knowing, growing knowledge dawned,
As time held hands
With me, the ever child,
Showing, mapped out, a new ecstatic starting.

Nature's Balm

There is no shame in the tears that fall.
They bathe the soul,
easing the pain of all that life throws at us.
They are the outward expression
of our innermost feelings.
God-given, silent, precious drops
speaking volumes.
A language understood by all,
from every race and creed.
Moving hearts as nothing else can.
Release for our anger,
balm for our sorrow or despair.
Giving us relief and the strength to go on.
They show the world we care.
And often, as they glisten upon swollen lids,
we suddenly look through them to see
the rainbow of a brighter day.

Forward Movement

When I say to you, "I'm really going through it at the moment", the very words imply motion and forward movement. I am not going over the top of the problem, or skirting round the edges, I am simply passing through. Not dwelling or abiding, staying or living, residing or lodging, but moving onward.

I take heart then, when trouble strikes, for I must, of necessity, come out the other side. Maybe I will be sadder, perhaps wiser, but certainly stronger than if I had never passed that way. Difficulties have shaped my character and given me the ability to face the next onslaught with the advantage of experience. Without problems to face and solve, mankind would still be living in the Dark Ages.

My Daughter

Loving you is easy,
I love the way you are,
for the start of that little smile
that tickles gently
at the corner of your mouth.
For the way your toss your head,
sometimes in defiance
and sometimes just for the sheer joy
of living and laughing.
I love you for your hard determination
to succeed against all odds,
and yet your soft understanding
when those around you fail.
For your love of life
and your coming to terms
with being a friend,
as well as a daughter.
But most of all because you are part of me,
conceived in longing, nurtured in love,
treasured above all else.
Yes, loving you is easy.

And I, your Mother

Precious new baby, unspoiled by age,
Unmarked and innocent, an unwritten page,
And I, your mother, so full of hope,
Through parenthood's jungle must grope.
I pray you will know you are cradled in love,
Wanted and longed for, all else above.

Adventurous toddler, learning so fast,
So many milestones already passed,
And I, your mother, by example must show,
In loving security which way you grow.
I pray for the patience to talk and to play,
Flowers of tomorrow are from seeds of today.

Questioning scholar, with choices galore,
Wanting to experiment, to know even more,
And I, your mother, my grip not so tight,
With patient tolerance must teach what is right.
I pray for the strength to stand up to the test,
And not follow blindly along with the rest.

Rebellious teenager, pulling away,
So easy to bruise, so easy to stray,
And I, your mother, waiting to share,
Yet knowing that all I can do is be there.
I pray for the insight to know when to act,
And when to behave with incredible tact.

Eager young adult, confident and changed,
Leaving the nest as nature arranged,
And I, your mother, must learn to let go,
Knowing you've learnt well all that I know.
I pray that you'll cope, keep ideals in sight,
Then at least I shall know I got some of it right!

*What we install
 into the memory bank
of a child can never be
 erased or deleted.*

A Thump in the Night

My partner snores, does yours?

Not soft gentle rustling

as a breeze through tall bamboo.

Or even the rushing noise

of a gale force wind

as it gathers momentum towards a storm.

Oh no, the noise resembles more

a herd of French wild boar,

at least one hundred in a group,

snorting in eagerness for miles

to find truffles

among the dead leaf piles.

I love my partner, except at night,

for then as the crescendo builds

into a deafening roar,

I could quite easily throttle him!

I lie rigid with emotion,
muscles tense, for sleep yearning,
an inner hatred burning.
I could quite happily sit on his head, instead
I thump him hard and shake his floppy arm,
until the noise abates and all is calm.
The ear splitting snores
you can hear through doors,
but when my sleepless night is done,
what does he say?
With croaking voice, deep and hoarse,
"I've had an awful night,
are you all right?"
Well, no I'm not, I'm in a snot,
and my partner's snores
are quite simply the cause!
How I long for a cure to the endless snore!

Insight

Look up
from all that you are doing,
and see the sunset,
birds on the wing
as evening darkens into night.

Look up
and see the brightness
of a brand new day,
as the sun rises upon another dawn,
so you can start again.

Look up
and see the smiling face
of a friend,
there for you when all seems lost,
with words of comfort and of love.

Look up
for then the way ahead
seems clearer
the path less hazardous,
a bright horizon full of future hope.

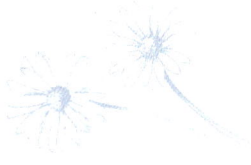

St Jude

Feast Day 28 October

Catholic tradition names St Jude as the Patron Saint of Lost Causes, or as I prefer to say, "hopeless cases"! In the New Testament he is described as a relative of Jesus. It is thought that the early Christians were afraid to offer prayers to St Jude, because of the similarity in name between him and Judas Iscariot, the disciple who betrayed Jesus in the Garden of Gethsemane. Supplicants only offered petitions to him when all other prayers had fallen on deaf ears, hence the "lost causes" title.

If you are like me, subject constantly to the irritations of Murphy's Law, then this is definitely the saint for you! Many times I have appealed for help, in situations where all hope appeared to be lost, and somehow, miraculously, something has happened to change things. When the chips are down and all seems lost, why not try it? If it works for me, it can work for you too.

Murphy's Law

It's operating here today, that dreaded Murphy's Law,
It happens Mondays without fail, I've seen it all before!
Alarm clock failed to waken me, cat mess upon the floor,
The dog has rolled in most of it, and spread it round some more!

Of course the toast lands fat side down, my hair just will not do,
And on the way out to the car, I've skidded on that pooh!
It's raining, so the wipers work, but only for a spell,
One falls off halfway down the road, so driving is sheer hell!

The boss is also in a flap, computer on the blink,
The phone lines never cease their ring, the copier's out of ink!
Just everyone is anti-me, lunchtime does not exist,
For I'm busy crossing items from the ever-growing list!

Yes, Murphy's Law is in full flow, arriving home at last,
There's been a major power cut, the fridge defrosting fast.
The dog is crossing all her legs, the cat is in a mood,
And as for me and Murphy's Law, I'm pleading to St Jude!

The Blessing of St Jude

*Now to him who is able to keep
you from falling and to present you
without blemish before the presence
of his glory with rejoicing,
to the only God, our Saviour
through Jesus Christ our Lord,
be glory, majesty, dominion
and authority,
before all time and now,
and forever.*

Amen.

Gossamer Threads

One morning just as dawn began to raise
The inky velvet drapes of lingering night,
I saw a sight that caused my hurried gaze
To stop and stare in wonder and delight.
In shimmering silver works of art there fell,
From branch to flower, woven from gate to post,
The lacy gossamer of each spider's spell,
All single yet one whole united host.

As people filled the quiet street with rush,
With bleary eyes still blind from sleep to see,
It took a moment's careless, thoughtless brush,
To break the strands of silken symmetry.
I marvelled as with speed and dextrous grace,
And not deterred by all that fate could send,
Each spider worked upon the broken lace,
The tattered remnants to enlarge and mend.

I could not help the lesson there to learn,
For though we think each one we stand apart,
Yet through all life at every twist and turn,
We interact and touch each other's heart.
The pattern of this personal design,
Is intricate and beautiful to see,
But when with other lives we intertwine,
Our love completes and joins the tapestry.

How careful then must be the moves we make,
To family friends and all we meet each day,
For angry words and hostile actions break
The delicate intended interplay.
But if in haste or thinking not we spoil,
Then like the spiders let us turn once more,
With silken threads of love make it our toil,
Returning glorious patterns as before.

*What we say to each
other matters.
For words, once spoken,
can never be unsaid.
They remain in the very
air we breathe,
like sharpened swords or
soothing salve.*

On Being Called Platitudinous!

I looked up the various meanings of that 'platitudinous' word,
Finding it means inane, inept, and really quite absurd!
I never thought of me like that, I honestly admit.
But virtue's in the rhyme that talks of wearing caps that fit!

I found some other meanings too, reading with just a smile,
Finding it means banality, unfruitful, not worthwhile!
I never thought of me like that, it gave me quite a turn.
But never mind, the saying goes, we all must live and learn!

In my thesaurus printed there I noted with trivial glee,
That I am hackneyed, stale and trite, full of vapidity!
I always thought of me as cute, intelligent, at ease.
Which proves to me beyond a doubt, I can't see wood for trees!

But never mind, I tell myself, God loves things great and small.
The mightier and cleverer, the farther is to fall!
If I am platitudinous my research must be wrong!
Perhaps to the accuser it must rightfully belong!

Consider all the platitudes contained within this verse,
All commonplace and hackneyed, much overworked and worse.
But …they are the English heritage, to use them can't be bad.
So you called me platitudinous and suddenly I'm glad!

The Leap of Faith

Upon a craggy windswept hill,
I watched with fearful glee,
Hang-gliders leaping off the edge,
With carefree certainty.
They seemed as though they never would,
From spiral plummet lift,
'Til thermals caught gay canopies,
And dangling they would drift.
The courage that it took to leap,
Had nothing to compare,
To the quiet peace of nature,
And their freedom in the air.

That scene reminds me that our Faith
Requires us to leap,
In confident assurance
That God will save and keep.
Our act of Faith He will reward
By raising us above
The sorrows of this earthly life,
In the thermals of His love.
The courage that it takes to leap,
Has nothing to compare,
To the peace and glorious freedom
Of living in His care.

Hugs

have a language all their own when words seem inadequate.
Ten sentiments a wordless hug can express:

1 *I love you very much* – you are so special

2 *I will miss you* – a lot

3 *Welcome back* – great to see you again

4 *I'm sorry* – can we still be friends?

5 *I sympathise* – I know how it feels

6 *Hang in there* – you will make it

7 *Congratulations* – you did it!

8 *Try not to worry* – it can't get much worse

9 *Good luck* – give it your best shot

10 *Thanks a million* – you are so generous

The Hug

I stood alone amid a crowd,
Where no one voiced a thought aloud.
No need for words as you drew near,
You hugged me close and made it clear
you understood.

The Vase

Displayed with pride upon my shelf,
With slightly crooked stance,
It's not a masterpiece and yet
Deserves a second glance.
You fashioned it with childish hands,
Uncertain how to mould,
Then painted it before you glazed,
In smudgy brown and gold.

You gave it to me guardedly,
Unsure about it's worth,
But I treasured it for all the love
Attendant at it's birth.
Since then you have perfected
The crafts wrought by your hands,
But that vase remains a symbol
Of a love that understands.

For all of us in some way
Are handicapped and spoiled,
And life has dealt us mighty blows,
Our best endeavours foiled.
We come to God quite guardedly,
Unsure about our worth,
But His love has never wavered
From the moment of our birth.

God looks past all our outward show
And sees beneath the glaze,
To our hidden depths of beauty
That can never be erased.
So that vase is a reminder
That appearances deceive.
God loves, despite the blemishes
We all of us receive.

Finding God

Finding God not just inside church walls
built by man,
as if to limit and contain
One so limitless.
Finding God not only in the vastness
of unending sky,
not simply in the roar of oceanic seas,
or desert's dryness.
Finding God not solely in the intellect
with concentrated thought,
or with persuasive argument
to justify.
But finding God inside our very being,
with hands held tight,
in every small routine of daily grind,
sharing this earthly life
with intimacy.

Witness

I saw in you the love of God,
That no distinction makes.
I saw in you the strength of God,
That life's hard trials can't break,
I saw in you the peace of God,
Born of utter trust,
I saw in you the joy of God,
With which your life is brushed.
And when I saw these things, I knew
That I could have them too.

Because of you the love of God,
Burns stronger in my life.
Because of you the strength of God,
Has helped me through my strife,
Because of you the peace of God,
Has stolen in on me.
Because of you the joy of God,
Has set my spirit free.
So now these gifts I saw in you,
In my life too are threaded through.

Each one of us has a specific task to complete whilst here on earth. If we omit to fulfil that obligation it remains undone for all eternity, for it does not appear on any other agenda except ours.

Marriage is:

making allowances

always being prepared to say sorry

realising the other person has needs

readjusting to change regularly

insisting on quality time together

acting as a team

growing together over the years

establishing a dialogue at all times

Warts and All

Living with someone is definitely not the same as simply knowing them, sharing the odd meal, or a visit to the theatre. When you live with someone you share the same space, day after day, for a considerable length of time. Suddenly those interesting little "warts" you noticed have become enormous growths! The quaint habits you laughed about and then dismissed, assume gigantic importance. The experts say that in any relationship, it is the minor irritations, the itching on a daily basis, that cause the most friction in any household; the hairs in the plug hole; the constant grime on the bathroom soap; regular sniffing or just the way that toast is eaten. All of these foibles and many, many more can suddenly ignite a flare up! It's no good trying to remove those "warts" surgically either. You simply have to look past them, keep your fingers crossed, and hope that the ones you have are no bigger than pimples.

Canine Perspective

I wish I could be what my dog thinks I am,
A hero in every degree,
A fearless commander, a leader of men,
A changer of history.
A sort of a saint with a halo so bright,
Provider of life's smallest need,
A ray of sunshine in the bleakness of life,
Paragon of virtue indeed.
The best kind of friend that could ever be found,
Reliable, straightforward, true,
Unselfish dispenser of time and concern,
Giving much more than is due.
A speedy forgiver when things go awry,
A judge who is utterly fair.
A person whose love can transcend every wrong,
Someone relied on to care.
For my dog sees past all the faults I possess,
And brings out the best I can be.
So if I could be what my dog thinks I am,
I would be a much better me!

Friendship

As summer spilling gently
into autumn's wealth,
our friendship grows.

Beyond spring with bubbling chatter,
and with newness rife,
from shallow root,
into a rich full-blossomed understanding trust,
upright and strong.

Long gone the clenched, closed tightness
of a forming bud,
hedged from the storm.

Now friendship flowers,
as deep and secret thoughts are shared,
open to view.
Two souls upon a journey we, rooted beside,
bonded in love.

*An acquaintance
is someone you can
laugh with.*

*A friend is someone
who won't laugh if you
sometimes need to weep.*

An Image of Thee

When I should be grateful
Help me to know it.
When I should be sorry
Help me to show it.
When asked for advice
Help me think twice.
When others walk away
Help me to stay.
So I may be
An image of Thee.

I'm Not Superstitious, Are You?

Don't walk in the cracks in the pavement,
Yelled my brother, in fear and alarm.
If you do, then the goblins will get you,
And you'll come to some terrible harm!
Well, I walked on the cracks in the pavement,
Then just as my shoe heel got stuck,
I found a round shiny penny,
Which I kept to give daylong good luck.
But… I'm not superstitious, are you?

Don't walk under any sort of ladders,
My mother would gently advise.
If you do, then bad luck will surround you,
It could signal your sudden demise!
Well, I walked under scaffold and ladders,
And suffered no ill will or more,
Though I tapped on the nearest wood three times
Then spat in the wind to make sure!
But… I'm not superstitious, are you?

Don't look at the full moon through glass dear,
My father reproached, looking sad,
If you do, then as sure as the sunrise,
You'll end up quite utterly mad!
Well, I looked through the window at midnight,
At the moon as it shone through the glass,
Whilst rapidly saying my rosary,
And hoping the madness would pass!
But… I'm not superstitious, are you?

Don't look when the ambulance drives past,
Or the magpies strut round, cried my friend,
If you do, then the fate you are tempting,
Will cause you to long for your end!
Well, I've watched as the ambulance wails by,
Seen the flash of a bird black and white,
But I wait for a black cat to pass me,
And so far I've managed all right!
So… I'm not superstitious, are you?

The Tapestry

I watched an old lady sit painstakingly filling in a canvas. Slowly she pulled the needle in and out of the stiff unyielding material. There was a grace in the movement of her ageing fingers, and a design of love filled in among the colours in the picture.

I stood behind her, unable to see the whole scene, peering with furrowed brow, wanting to make some sense of my fractured vision. She rose and moved away from the tapestry.

"You see," she said, "understanding is easier when viewed from a distance. Each piece is woven at each stage but only when it is complete can we see the meaning of what seems meaningless during the making."

How like our lives is that tapestry. The interwoven stitches of experience sometimes seeming to make no sense at all. Yet, in it all there is a master design, completed when the Maker of our personal tapestry has finished. Only then will we see its true glory; the purpose behind every keen stitch that pierced through our lives, without obvious reason and without apparent plan. In the meantime, we can rest in the knowledge that we are not alone throughout the making.

No Strings Attached

Pure gift is what He gives,
dependent not on deeds we do,
that oh, so righteous seem.
Unearned this gift of love,
no strings attached.
Though still unworthy, yet
we reach with eagerness,
our barren souls yearning
for love.

He waits, our God, listening
for our feeble cries,
that bring us back to Him.
At once we are redeemed,
no strings attached.
For love is freely given,
sin wiped from memory, gone,
traceless and erased
in love.

Be joyful then that He, Creator,
names us, belonging thus,
sinful and flawed but still
loved utterly, at once,
no strings attached.
Trying only as we journey here,
in our poor human state,
to mirror in some small way
His love.

Gratitude

I thought I had nothing to be thankful for,

until I saw a man with no legs,

as I ran to catch the bus.

I thought I was poor,

until I saw a beggar in a doorway,

as I hurried past with my shopping.

I thought I was hungry,

until I saw the refugees scratching in dirt,

as I watched the news on television.

I thought I was misunderstood,

until I saw the Cross on Calvary,

as I knelt alone in a church one day.

I thought I was lonely,

until I realised that God was watching

and waiting for my friendship.

Gifts from Above

I can hardly remember the gifts I received for Christmas three years ago. Or now, aged over 50, what brought me joy on my 23rd birthday. Yet I can remember with uncanny clarity the unexpected encounters with nature; the owl caught in the torch glow on a dark night, eyes like amber traffic lights and fluffy body stunned into stillness. I think with awe of the wantonness of the waves crashing onto a December shore and the sound of their cold fury; the thrilling perfection of a summer rose, glistening with dew as morning breaks.

These gifts are what my subconscious holds forever in loving awareness. For they are given to me as sudden, unexpected gifts of love.

These remembered moments are the times when I catch my breath and see for just a second, the greatness of my God.

The Candlelight of Prayer

I stood upon a far-off hill,
In a world beyond my own,
Wondering at the light that shone,
As I gazed there all alone.
It seemed a dream, yet, oh, so real,
As I watched bright spirals rise,
And heard the silence broken
By a myriad of sighs.

I felt a hand so gently touch,
Startled, I turned to see
An illuminated figure,
In the emptiness round me.
Questioning I spoke and said,
"Whence come these plumes of light,
That brighten up the darkness,
Bearing sighs that fill the night?"

Softly then the voice replied,
It was filled with sweetest love,
"The light comes from the candles lit,
Below for those above.
The sighs you hear, unspoken prayers,
Reaching the Father's ear,
So He can hold lost loved ones close,
And all whom earth hold dear."

The moment passed, I could not tell,
Whose was the loving voice.
He turned to go, but even then,
I felt my heart rejoice.
On His feet as He walked away,
I saw the Cross-marks there,
And knew that souls were safely kept,
In the candlelight of prayer.

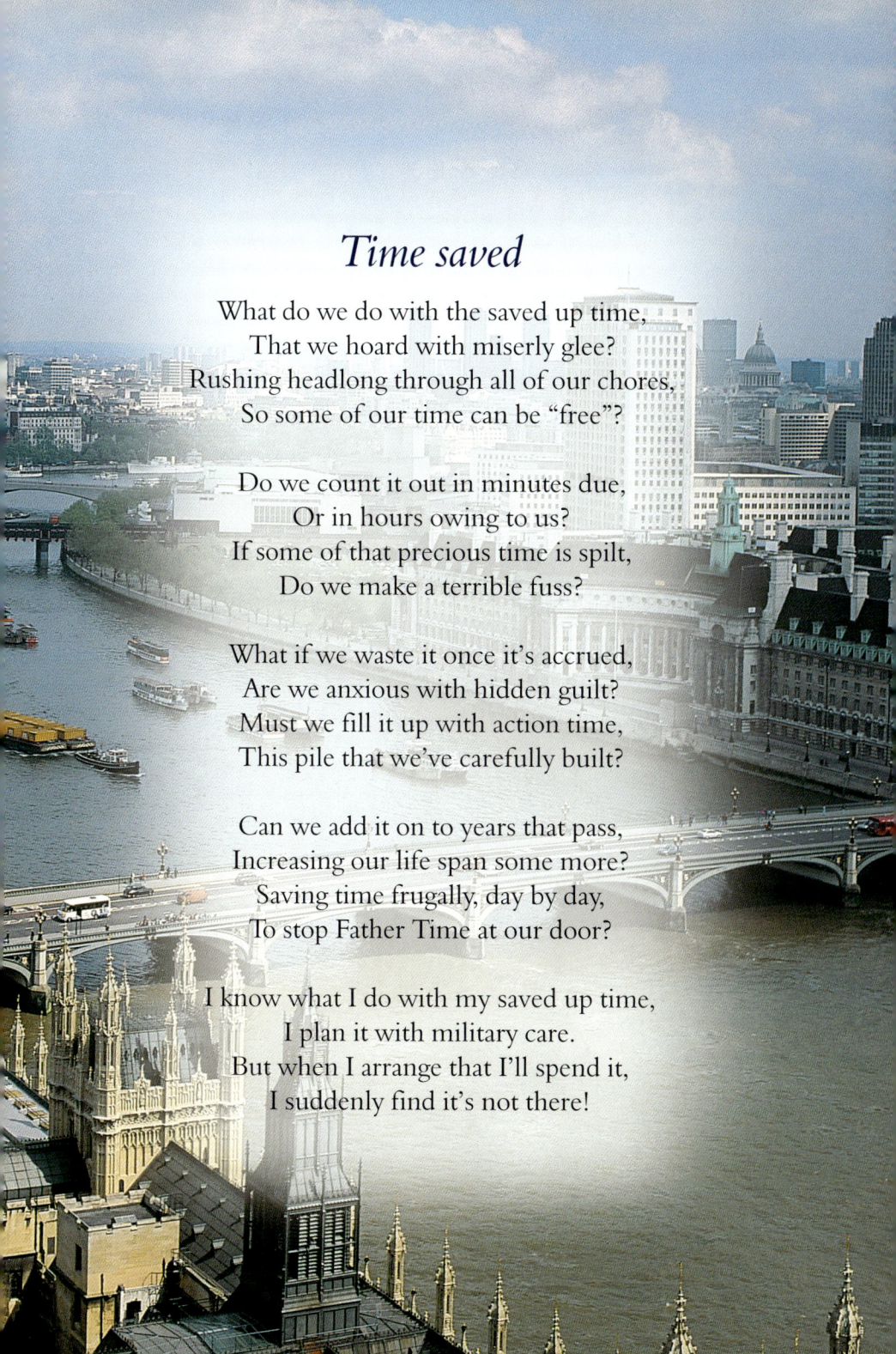

Time saved

What do we do with the saved up time,
That we hoard with miserly glee?
Rushing headlong through all of our chores,
So some of our time can be "free"?

Do we count it out in minutes due,
Or in hours owing to us?
If some of that precious time is spilt,
Do we make a terrible fuss?

What if we waste it once it's accrued,
Are we anxious with hidden guilt?
Must we fill it up with action time,
This pile that we've carefully built?

Can we add it on to years that pass,
Increasing our life span some more?
Saving time frugally, day by day,
To stop Father Time at our door?

I know what I do with my saved up time,
I plan it with military care.
But when I arrange that I'll spend it,
I suddenly find it's not there!

Sometimes in life you have to take risks, decide tentatively what to do with a set of given circumstances and that is never easy. However, if you stay under the rock then nothing bad will happen but nothing good will either. So come out from under that rock where you hide in seeming safety and see the world; face the challenge head on. Maybe you will fail in some things you have set your heart on, but you might just succeed and therein lies the fun of finding out.

So don't despair if this time you didn't get it just right, because fortunately life gives us more than one chance, more than one occasion to shine. Life is about picking oneself up, starting again, moving onward. Always with hope, sometimes with excitement, but never with complete despair. For round each corner, far away from the seeming safety of the rock, there may be a golden opportunity lurking, just waiting for you alone to seize it and succeed.

Experience

How can I appreciate good health,

Unless I have experienced illness?

How can I measure another's pain,

Unless I have suffered my own?

How can I enjoy laughter,

Until I've had cause to cry?

How can I value my friends,

Until I have been alone?

How can I know security,

Until I have felt afraid?

How can I recognise the good times,

Unless I have been through what's bad?

How can I expect to be loved,

Unless I have loved in return?

In the bank account of life over a term of 70 years, the number of days available to spend is approximately 25,567.

Wise investment is essential, as interest is accrued on a daily basis in Eternity.

Job's Story

Job thought he was so saintly,
Living in the land of Uz,
A man who hated evil,
But perfection made him buzz.
He had his share and more than most,
Of cattle, ox and sheep,
And strapping sons, and daughters
Who all kept him from his sleep.

But though Job always praised his God,
His kids began to drift.
They drank too much and ate too much,
Which made Job rather miffed!
To save them from the wrath of God,
Job offered every day,
For each a sacrifice to God,
A price he had to pay.

But Satan walked among them,
And his plan was plain to see,
He wanted all their souls to keep,
Until eternity.
He mocked Job's God, who walked there too,
"If Job was poor," he said,
"And all the troubles of this world
Fell down upon his head…

Guess what I bet he'd curse you then,
And stop his endless praise.
Because it's easy to be perfect
When all blessings fill your days."
So God gave his permission
For the Devil's upperhand,
To wreak his personal vengeance,
All around Job's fruitful land.

He killed the sheep and oxen
And the servants all demised,
But Job still kept on praising God,
Though somewhat mystified!
Then Satan, seeing all this fail,
Increased his wretched plot,
Attacking Job with boils and germs,
He rained on him the lot!

Then Job was sore beside himself,
And took himself away,
He sat in dirt and ashes,
Lamenting all the day.
He cursed the day that he was born,
And wished that he was dead.
He could not comprehend why God
Heaped troubles on his head.

"For after all," he said in peek,
"I've been a Godly man.
This surely is not just reward,
For doing all I can?"
For days and days Job argued thus,
He felt he'd lived in vain.
What use was there in being good,
If nought there was to gain?

His friends all came to visit him,
Voicing the current view,
They said, "you must be full of sin,
For God to punish you."
But Job denied sin utterly,
Yet still he could not see
Why God had just deserted him,
In all his misery.

A desolation filled his soul,
His strength had all but failed,
When through the whirlwind's mighty roar,
The voice of God assailed.
He chided Job, for it was clear,
In His Almighty plan
When earth was formed and all was new,
He had not need of man.

Then God asked Job if he could think
Of any single thing,
Over which Job had dominion,
Instead of God the King.
Then Job inside his heart was sad,
For suddenly he saw
He had not really known his God
As he had thought before.

He realised when in greatest need,
Alone and in despair,
The seeming hiddenness of God,
Did not preclude His care.
Job found a closer walk with God,
Through suffering offered up,
The strength to carry on despite
The bitterness of cup.

But the story ended happily,
For God restored Job's health,
And friends brought gold and silver,
Thus increasing all his wealth.
He had a load more children
And with ox and ass galore,
He lived a long and happy life,
Much better than before.

Forgiveness

When you look at me, don't only see
My sometimes bungling inadequacy.
The times I try so hard and yet,
My efforts seem to you inept.
But see instead the love therein,
That wells and streams from deep within.

When listening to me, don't just hear
The syntax that might not seem clear,
When jumbled thoughts and words combine
To accidentally undermine.
But note the good intentions there,
That tells your heart I really care.

And if by chance or thoughtless word,
I seem to you to be absurd,
Relationships are all but spent,
Despite my very best intent,
Then let us find some common ground,
To start again the next time round.

*In order to be forgiven,
we must first learn
to be forgiving.*

*In order to truly forgive,
we must also learn
to be forgetful.*

What's in a Number?

I may be old, I may be grey,
I may be past my prime,
But I can match you youngsters,
At any given time!

For I can surf the Internet,
And Gameboys are a breeze,
The mobile phone holds little dread,
I email as I please!

I exercise with confidence,
I cycle to my work,
And as for Nature's remedies,
They give me quite a perk!

I have the added edge on youth,
It is so plain to see,
I've done with acne, spills and thrills,
I'm happy to be me!

I may look old, I may look grey,
But I'm glad to be alive,
For on the inside looking out,
I feel just twenty-five!

Full Circle

When I was just about five,
I couldn't wait to get on those swings.

When I was just about ten,
I couldn't wait to start middle school.

When I was just about fifteen,
I couldn't wait to get a job.

When I was just about twenty,
I couldn't wait to get married.

When I was just about twenty five,
I couldn't wait to have kids.

When I was just about thirty,
I couldn't wait for those kids to grow up.

When I was just about thirty five,
I couldn't wait to get a job again.

When I was just about forty,
I couldn't wait for my kids to get married.

When I was just about forty five,
I couldn't wait for some grandchildren.

Now I am just about fifty,
I can't wait to get on those swings again!

The Gift of Foster Parents

Although you're not my parents
In the natural way of things,
And you never had the pleasure
That a newborn baby brings,
Yet you gave to me a precious gift
That came straight from your heart,
A home and a belonging,
With the chance of a fresh start.

Although you're not my parents
In the scientific sense,
And the problems that accompanied me,
Were almost too intense,
Yet you gave to me a precious gift,
That money cannot buy,
A love that through my stormy years,
Refused to shrink or die.

Although you're not my parents
As the law would clearly state,
And I came to you half-used, half-grown,
Unsure about my fate,
Yet you gave to me a precious gift
One I shall always treasure,
You showed me God and his great love,
That we can never measure.

So to me you are my parents,
In a very special way,
And it matters not what people,
Or the world at large may say.
I thank you for the gifts you gave,
And all the things you do,
But most of all I thank the Lord,
For sending me to you.

A Prayer at Work

Lord, help me to keep my eyes open, my mouth shut, and my brain in gear.

A Prayer for Help

Lord, please help me in this situation, and if it's not possible to change it, then help me change my attitude towards it.

A Family Prayer at Night

Lord, bless us and keep us in your safety and care this night. May no harm come to any of us and nothing frighten us. Send your guardian angels down to watch over us whilst we sleep, and bring us safely and in good health to the morning light.

Amen.

Retirement Prayer

Allow me Lord, the time to cogitate,
But not stagnate.
To walk untrodden paths with glee,
In company.

Grant me a mind that still is crystal clear,
And free from fear.
Courage to capture dreams of yesterday,
Without delay.

Allow me Lord, the time to take my ease,
Free from disease.
Supply sufficient not for want, but need,
Minus all greed.

And with the passing time, nurture in me,
A love of Thee.
So I, when moving from this earthly plane,
With Thee remain.

Practise to Make Perfect

Practise laughing when you feel down,
A smile is easier than a frown,
It costs less effort in the end,
And certainly will make a friend.
Practise thinking of happy things,
When suddenly a bad mood springs,
We each have power to change our thought,
Control our mind and then re-sort.
Practise sometimes living the now,
Not tomorrow, the when and how,
Living each moment with a zest,
Treating each minute as your best.
Practise talking to those you meet,
For them it could be their only treat,
Nod a greeting as you pass by,
It works much better than a sigh.
Practise makes perfect so they say,
And slowly you'll notice day by day,
Positive thinking casts out doubt,
You'll find you've spread some joy about.

Laughter

- ⭐ reduces stress by depressing the release of the hormone serum corticol, which is released in abundance when we start to become stressed.

- ⭐ increases our immunity to respiratory disease by producing immunoglobulin, an antibody that fights this type of infection.

- ⭐ helps us to tolerate pain more effectively.

- ⭐ uses fewer muscles than it does to frown.

- ⭐ is highly contagious to anyone in close proximity. Contaminate wantonly!

- ⭐ helps us to keep the world in perspective and to relate to other people.

- ⭐ defuses hostile situations - it is impossible to be angry and laugh at the same time.

Jonah's Story

It wasn't that Jonah was awkward,
But just that he failed to see,
Why God should demand such a service,
From someone as busy as he.
For God in His infinite wisdom,
Had planned that poor Jonah should go,
To Nineveh, city of evil,
The ways of the good Lord to show.

But Jonah made plans that were better,
To escape from the Lord was his wish.
He hastened himself to the harbour,
And hopped on a boat to Tarshish.
But the journey had not long continued,
When mariners raised the alarm.
A ferocious storm had engulfed them,
They feared they would all come to harm.

Then panic and fear spread quite quickly,
Each prayed to his God with grim dread,
All of them, that is, barring Jonah,
Who lay fast asleep in his bed.
They soon put a stop to his slumber,
By hauling him up on the deck,
Asking to explain all his motives,
And how they could stop a shipwreck.

"Throw me to the sea," cried out Jonah,
For he knew that the fault was his own.
So they did and the storm was abated,
But Jonah felt awfully alone.
He cried out to God as he sank down,
With waves billowing over his head.
He asked God's protection, forgiveness,
But a whale gulped his body instead.

Well, Jonah was in that whale's belly,
For all of three days and three nights,
But God in his Almighty wisdom,
Still had Nineveh set in His sights.
He caused that poor whale indigestion,
So it threw Jonah up on the shore,
Again God repeated His order,
Exactly the same as before.

This time Jonah listened intently,
Then travelled long miles to get there,
To Nineveh, city of evil,
To warn all the people, beware.
The days they had left were just forty,
To turn back to God and repent,
If not then the whole of the city,
Would be wasted, flattened and spent.

So they fasted in sackcloth and ashes,
Repenting in utter despair,
Then God in His mercy had pity,
Saving all the souls that were there.
But Jonah was not very happy,
He felt that he'd wasted his time,
What good was there in his great journey,
If God forgave Nineveh's crime?

He sat in a sulk by the city,
The sun searing down on his head,
For God had reneged on his promise,
Not a single person was dead.
The Lord sent an eggplant to shade him,
In order to help with his grief,
And Jonah was glad of such refuge,
'Til a worm came and ate every leaf.

Then Jonah was madder than ever,
His thought was he might as well die,
For now he had nothing to save him,
From the sun beating down in the sky.
Poor Jonah had lost it completely,
For as God pointed out, there and then,
Can an eggplant be much more important,
Than Nineveh's thousands of men?

The story of Jonah is ended,
But the lesson is plain to us all,
The forgiveness of God is not stingy,
No matter how greatly we fall.
No sin is too great for redemption,
It takes just a brief change of heart,
The moment we're sorry, God's ready,
To offer us all a fresh start.

Alone But Not Lonely

No one can measure another's pain,
No one can really feel.
Alone we bear it time and again,
Seeming never to heal.
Others will say that they understand,
Knowing the grief we bear,
But they feel it only second-hand,
It isn't their despair.
But there are unseen hands that guide,
Holding with tender love,
Someone sharing, standing beside,
Sending help from above.
So when you feel that no one will care,
Just how much you endure,
Turn and you'll glimpse His presence there,
Waiting to reassure.

Receiving Graciously

When you are a giver by nature, the hardest lesson to learn is to be a gracious receiver. During my periods of illness and hardship, I found that the most difficult aspect of it all. I have always been fiercely independent and considered that particular part of my personality as being an asset rather than a disadvantage. I wrongly assumed that I achieved most things with a little help from God! It wasn't until I was brought to my knees by illness and financial hardship, that it dawned on me that the reverse was true. God actually achieved all things with just a little help from me!

Looking at it in terms of my faith, I realised that my very independence had been a stumbling block in my growth as a Christian. If I couldn't allow other people to assist me, and be gracious and humble in accepting that assistance, then I probably wasn't allowing God to do so either. The most important truth I learnt during my darkest, pain-filled moments was, that in order to become closer to God, I must first submit to Him completely, acknowledging my own inability to cope alone.

It was when I was at my weakest and most vulnerable, that I felt closest to God. For this reason I consider all that I have suffered, as being a blessing rather than a hindrance and would gladly suffer it again in order to feel the very real presence of God in my life, as I did at that time.

My Glimpse of Eternity

At first I thought it was a dream,
slipping so effortlessly
from the earth-bound part of me.
The shell of muscle, sinew, bone,
all I had known,
no longer trapped, but free.
Not floating in some magical,
imaginary moment,
but feeling feet treading,
hands touching,
sight seeing.

When your turn comes, don't be afraid.
It is the same,
without the pain,
the very best of all we know now.
Filled with family, friends,
all who have earlier travelled,
senses still sharp,
everything focused,
knowledge acquired.

All around us on a different plane
exists this world, and souls
from earth's restrictions freed,
support and interact with us.
So close are those we love
that fingers touch,
and messages brush gently
through our thoughts, to teach, not terrify.
This life is part of all that is,
nothing is lost,
just changed
and we continue on.

Grieve not too long for those you love,
thinking them gone,
for they are here, all around you.
As guardian angel souls,
they keep watch over those they love,
as you in turn,
will do for those you love.

Epilogue

This life is only a journey towards eternity. Along the way we will all meet with sorrow and with joy; with friends and with enemies; with those who bring out the best in us and those who do not. Many people in the travelling will wonder from time to time, what this life is all about or maybe why they should bother at all. If you believe that this life is all there is and dying simply means total extinction, then it matters not how you live. But if you believe, as I do, that this life is a preparation ground, a training school for the next stage of the journey to God, then it does indeed become a matter of life or death.

We are all offered the chance to begin or to continue our relationship with God here and now, for who knows what tomorrow may bring. Millions of us take out policies that cover us for theft, for loss of earnings and for so called "acts of God", but how many more millions refuse to take out the best policy there is, one without small print and with no hidden charges? There are no forms to be filled in, no exemption clauses and no catches. Faith in God gives us the assurance that this life is not all there is and when this life ends, a better one begins.

An abridged autobiography!

The poems in this book reflect the inspiration I have taken from my life and the experiences and opportunities it has offered me.

My early childhood was spent in a children's home. At the age of nine I was fostered by a Methodist minister and his wife, whom I later cared for through cancer and heart disease. After attending boarding school in Hertfordshire, I trained as a nurse in London before working as a staff nurse in Norwich. Always ready for a new challenge, I re-trained as a secretary at the age of 49 and thoroughly enjoyed studying and passing exams with youngsters half my age.

I have enjoyed a long and happy marriage and have two lovely daughters. The anguish I felt when my elder daughter emigrated to the States was soon replaced by a sense of comfort and pride that she was making her own unique journey through life – just like her mother!

My faith has provided me with great strength throughout the difficult times – my own batttle with severe ill health and the financial hardship my husband and I endured in the 1990s when, as a result of the recession, he was made redundant and we nearly lost our family home.

Throughout these varied experiences I have continued to learn and grow spiritually, enjoying the uncomplicated pleasures of nature, of God and of those I love.

Each day presents us all with great possibilities and in this book I sincerely hope you will find something that will help you as you travel through life.